This book belongs to

Includes 50 coloring designs from Selina's Fantasy Art Coloring Books-

Enchanted - Magical Forests Coloring Collection
Fairy Art Coloring Book
Fairy Companions Coloring Book

As an artist, color is a thing of magic in my life. Color creates shapes, forms, and feelings in the artworks I paint. Laying color onto a blank page is when I feel closest to true magic, when I feel happiest and most relaxed, and it's through what I create that I share my love of magic with the world. Through my coloring books I want to share that same magic with you.

The artworks in my books are based on my completed paintings, which I have painted over the last ten years as a professional artist. I have created the coloring designs to be a mix of intricate and detailed while still fun and accessible. There is something for lovers of meditative detail while simple enough to not be overwhelming for younger colorists. ~ *Selina*

See the colors the artist chose for her paintings at www.selinafenech.com

Magical Minis - Pocket Sized Fantasy Art Coloring Book by Selina Fenech
First Published November 2015
Second Edition Published October 2016
Published by Fairies and Fantasy PTY LTD
ISBN: 978-0-9943554-5-4

Artworks Copyright © 2000-2016 Selina Fenech
All rights reserved.

No part of this book may be reproduced in any form or by any electronic or mechanical means including information storage and retrieval systems, known now or hereafter invented, without permission in writing from the creator. The only exception is by a reviewer, who may share short excerpts in a review.

Using This Book

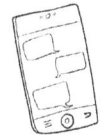

Turn off and move away from distractions. Relax into the peaceful process of coloring and enjoy the magic of these fantasy images.

This book works best with color pencils or markers. Wet mediums should be used sparingly. Slip a piece of card behind the image you're working on in case the markers bleed through.

Take this book with you for coloring on the go! It's designed to be small and light enough to be portable.

Never run out of fantasy coloring pages by signing up to Selina's newsletter. Get free downloadable pages and updates on new books at -
selinafenech.com/free-coloring-sampler/

Share Your Work

Share on Instagram with **#colorselina** to be included in Selina's coloring gallery, and visit the gallery for inspiration.

selinafenech.com/coloringgallery

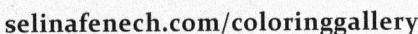

About the Artist

As a lover of all things fantasy, Selina has made a living as an artist since she was 23 years old selling her magical creations. Her works range from oil paintings to oracle decks, dolls to digital scrapbooking, plus Young Adult novels, jewelry, and coloring books.

Born in 1981 to Australian and Maltese parents, Selina lives in Australia with her husband and daughter. She loves food, gardening, geekery and all things magical.

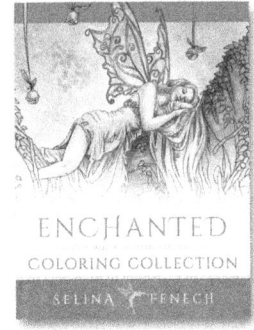

See all books online at - viewAuthor.at/sfcolor

www.ingramcontent.com/pod-product-compliance
Ingram Content Group UK Ltd.
Pitfield, Milton Keynes, MK11 3LW, UK
UKHW021323180426
11947UKWH00017B/1391